Wholistic Health Made Easy

Dedicated to my four children, who continuously inspire.

Zachariah, Sarah, Aubrey and Wallace

Physical

Water, Hydration

Nutrition, Stillness- Breath-

Healing Crisis

Emotional

The Emotional Body Construct

Principles of Transmutation

The Three Powers

Mental

Transmutation and Visualization

Laws of Light

Spiritual

Meditation

Creating a Sacred Space

Second Printing- Spring 2018

Wholistic health and self-healing~

Author's Note~

The wholistic model may be simplistically defined as the interconnection of the physical, emotional, mental and spiritual energies within all life.

Each of these aspects is governed by natural principles, in which we operate individually and interdependently. This book contains an introduction to practical applications for conscious evolution and self-healing within a wholistic construct. Some definitions of the 'healing crisis' are included. Understanding how a healing crisis affects the physical, emotional, mental and spiritual bodies is of great importance in the self-healing process. I have condensed complex information for the application of a healthy lifestyle.

The information in this book is for educational purposes only. It is in no way intended to treat, nor to diagnose, cure or prescribe.

Let's Get Physical

Physical energy is the end expression in the wholistic spectrum of creation. Physical creation begins in spirit (energy), comes through the mental body (thought/vision), through the emotional body into the physical form. Physical principles support steadfast movement through emotional resistance, mental polarities and spiritual unconsciousness. In this way we evolve, harmonizing with natural law. The following is a practical outline to an evolutionary approach that works from the physical level up. The physical foundation facilitates emotional opening which facilitates access to the mental body, then spiritual, in this order. Nutrition (all things consumed), conscious breathing and stillness are three principles from where we begin our physical revitalization.

Water - Crystals of Life

Providing the internal environment where watery bodies may thrive is paramount to wholistic health. The first on the list of importance is hydration. Find the best spring water source available. Hydrate sufficiently each day as top priority.

- Staying hydrated; One half the body's weight in ounces of water per day, compensating for dehydrating effects of caffeine, alcohol, herbal teas, exercise, diuretics etc. is considered minimal hydration.

- 150 lbs body weight= 75 oz. water per day

When the body becomes chronically dehydrated, the thirst mechanism shuts down. As we provide sufficient hydration consistently over a period of time, a natural thirst will return.

The Bodies Many Cries for Water –

Dr. Batmanghelidj is an excellent book on hydration and health.

Water is acutely affected by emotional energy, thought and sound. Love, Gratitude and Forgiveness brings water into a cohesive structure. This cohesiveness then has the ability to communicate more clearly. With continuous and sufficient hydration, we lay the most important physical foundation for a healthy wholistic life.

The Hidden Messages In Water, by Dr. Emoto gives a more thorough explanation of these principles. "Pollution originated within our own consciousness. We started to think we wanted a bountiful and convenient lifestyle at any cost, and this selfishness led to the pollution of the environment that now affects every corner of the globe."

Dr. Masaru and Kazuko Emoto

Be Still and Breath

Stillness-

Being still may be the most important physical activity we choose. Sit or lay in stillness, gently holding spine straight, with no voluntarily movement while breathing deep and even without pause. These two simple physical practices- stillness and conscious breath allow access to the emotional body with nutritional support.

Three part breath-

Sit comfortably with the spine held straight. In a clean outdoor environment is optimum, yet for daily practice an alter space with a wool blanket is fine. Through the nostrils breathe deeply into the abdomen, filling the lungs from the bottom up until at full capacity. Let the belly expand. Exhale evenly, through the nostrils from the top down pulling the abdomen in tightly at the end of the exhale. Do not pause between inhalation and exhalation- a smooth and steady flow. Making time each day to practice conscious breathing is helpful to bring increases oxygen to cells. This may strengthen the spine where the flow of cerebral spinal fluid affects the whole system.

Alternate nostril breathing~

Rest thumbs on either side of nostrils, with the third fingers touching slightly at top of head. Press right thumb on nostril and breathe deeply and evenly through left nostril while counting to 12. Press thumbs on both nostrils and hold breath while counting to 12. Release thumb from right nostril and exhale evenly while counting to 12, pull abdomen in at the end of the exhale. Do not pause at end of exhalation, go directly into inhalation. Inhale through right nostril to 12. Press right thumb, hold breath to a count of 12, release left thumb and exhale from left nostril. Breathe in left nostril at a count of 12. Twelve rounds practiced twice daily. Count one round each time you inhale from right nostril. At the end of the twelfth inhalation through right nostril, release pressure on both nostrils and exhale completely through both nostrils. Breathe deeply through both nostrils, exhaling completely x 12.

When our nutrition is working to revitalize, adding stillness and conscious breathing practices strengthens the spine which in turn opens the pranic channels (subtle energy system). This creates the environment for expanding inner awareness. From here consciousness may be accessed and changed. Emotional suppression comes forth to be transmuted. With continuous practice in emotional clearing, the mental body will be accessed for its edification. The spiritual shroud in which the physical, emotional and mental bodies are contained is accessed in increments upon the continuous evolution of the inner environment. This is the basis of the wholistic construct.

When practicing stillness, breath and emotional transmutation, create a sacred private space. Please do not use 'yoga mats'. They disconnect the electromagnetics of the earth, and are environmentally unfriendly.

The bath is an excellent option. One I have used for many years.

"Healing Crisis"

Hering's Law of Cure has been accepted for many years as the basic definition of the "healing crisis". This concept has been accepted by Natural Health Practitioners the world over including Chiropractic Physicians, Naturopaths, Homeopaths, Herbalists, Iridologists and a host of other valid natural health modalities.

HERING'S LAW OF CURE:

"All cure starts from within out, from the head down and in reverse order as the symptoms have appeared."

Since the introduction of Body Electronics in the 1960's, an expanded definition of the "Healing Crisis" has been offered.

'A healing crisis will begin with the willingness to do so, when an individual is ready both physiologically and psychologically. The basic foundation for healing crisis is nutritional. A healing crisis will begin from within out, in reverse order chronologically as to how the symptoms have appeared, tempered by the intensity of the trauma (physical- emotional- mental- spiritual). Poor nutrition over long periods is a trauma in itself. We process trauma of least severity (whatever we are ready and willing to process in that moment of time) is how the healing crisis unfolds. See emotional and mental transmutation in this booklet. For deeper understanding see The Body Electronics Experience, and the Logic In Sequence series by John Whitman Ray.

A healing crisis creates a hyper activity (intensification of symptoms), making it seem worse before getting better. Simple principle- what may get you into the healing crisis may assist to get you through it. In other words, during a HC, continue the nutritional and emotional transmutation throughout. It is often a difficult thing to determine a HC from a disease crisis. Always err on the side of caution.

Nutritional Foundation

1. Enzymes- Raw Protein- Amino Acids

These three work interdependently within the body. Enzymes are necessary for digestion and assimilation of nutrients, carbohydrates/sugars, fats and proteins. Raw protein digested efficiently provides the nutritional profile for the production of nine essential amino acids. When provided, the other nonessential amino acids may be synthesized within the body. This provides the endocrine system the necessary nutrition for the production of hormones. When stress is put on one endocrine gland, the effects are felt throughout the system, effecting hormonal production and balance. The modern diet may consist of a bombardment of sugars, fats etc., where our pancreas is under constant stress to provide necessary enzymes. Supplementation of high quality enzymes may assist to ease this digestive stress, eventually allowing for physical regeneration.

- Enzymes and raw protein provide the nutrition for the formation of amino acids, precursor to hormone production.
- Protein does not perform its function unless broken down into amino acids. Hence the importance of sufficient enzyme activity. Enzymes help extract chelated minerals from food. Enzymes transform chelated minerals into an alkaline detoxifying agent which combines with acid cellular wastes and toxic settlements within the body assisting to neutralize, preparing them for elimination.
- Raw bee pollen- preferably from a local apiary, digests efficiently by crushing and taking with a little honey.
- Many bean sprouts are good sources of raw protein.
- Two of 9 essential amino acids, tryptophan and lysine, are destroyed by heating/cooking at approximately 110 degrees F.
- Proteins, sugars and fats may require supplemented enzymes to digest efficiently.

Hormones act within the body as a catalyst in every metabolic function, endothermic and exothermic reactions which are necessary for biological transmutation; to heal and regenerate tissues and to warm or cool the body (healthy thyroid function).

2. Minerals & Trace Minerals

The body requires minerals to come from plants, or fossilized sea beds providing the extraction process does not damage the natural qualities. Minerals combine with enzymes makes an alkaline agent which neutralizes the acid metabolic by-products of the cells and other toxic conditions within the body and prepares them for elimination.

"The acid-alkaline balance (pH) of the tissue fluid is controlled by minerals." John Ray ND Minerals are essential for electrical catalyst within the body. Liquid minerals and mineral caps may be purchased online though Enzymes International. A readily available liquid trace mineral product called Concentrace is a good start.

Minerals
Written by Dr. John Ray ND

1. According to Senate Document No. 264, the official publication, 99 percent of American people are deficient in minerals, and a marked deficiency in any one of the more important minerals actually results in disease.

2. The body is equipped to chelate only a small amount of some inorganic elements from nature. Therefore, the body requires the minerals to come from plants in a chelated form that the minerals may be properly assimilated and utilized. The efficiency of each mineral is enhanced by balanced amounts of the others.

3. The body must maintain an adequate mineral supply to maintain a balance between internal and external pressures of the cells called osmotic equilibrium. This state must be maintained for normal cell function and continued youthful health.

4. All nutrients such as vitamins, proteins, enzymes, amino acids, carbohydrates, fats, sugars, oils, etc. require minerals for activity. All

bodily processes depend upon the action of minerals.

5. Trace chelated minerals are more important in nutrition than vitamins. Vitamins can be synthesized by living matter, minerals cannot.

6. Vitamins are required for every biochemical activity of the body. Vitamins cannot function unless minerals are present.

7. Minerals are the catalysts that make enzyme functions possible. Chelated minerals combine with enzymes into an alkaline detoxifying agent which neutralizes the acid metabolic by-products of the cells and other toxic conditions within the body and prepares them for elimination.

8. Hormonal secretion of glands is dependent upon mineral stimulation.

3. Essential Fatty Acids - EFA's-

Fats the body requires. Essential fatty acids are required for the development and function of the human brain, especially in the young.

"EFAs are especially necessary for proper function of the vision, nervous system, adrenal glands, and testes, playing a vital role in sperm formation and conception. Dr. Johanna Budwig, a German M.D. and biochemist, discovered that the blood of cancer patients was deficient in EFAs. a yellow-green pigment was found in place of the normal red blood pigment or hemoglobin. Along with certain dietary improvements, she gave her patients one and a half ounces (45 ml) or more of fresh flax oil as a means of getting EFAs into the body (flax oil is 55-65% Omega 3 and 15-25% Omega 6). The flax oil was consumed in combination with various dairy products, organic cottage cheese works well to provide the sulfur proteins which Budwig considered necessary for the EFAs to be properly utilized by the body. On this program, which included no other supplements, she found that within three months the yellow-green was replaced by red blood pigment". Douglas Morrison- Author of How We Heal

- Fats and oils are best consumed with food for proper assimilation.
  - Some healthy fats- Organic: hemp, avocado oil, quality butter, flax oil (provided it is fresh and kept cool).
  - Unhealthy fats- GMO canola, palm oil, soy (margarine).

Essential Fatty Acids and Dietary Fats by Douglas W. Morrison

Fats that Heal, Fats that Kill by Udo Erasmus
Nourishing Traditions by Sally Fallon
Nutrition and Physical Degeneration by Weston Price

1. There are two essential fatty acids or EFAs; these essential nutrients have been shown by leading researchers to be necessary for both the optimum health of the body as well as for freedom

from degenerative disease. They are known as Omega 3 (alpha-linolenic acid or ALNA) and Omega 6 (linoleic acid or LA).

2. In addition to these two EFAs, there are certain derivatives of each that some people do not produce in adequate amounts themselves so as to meet their own needs. Therefore, some people will also require a dietary source of these EFA derivatives as well. Biochemical individuality is an important concept to comprehend in this regard. (Refer to *Biochemical Individuality* by Roger Williams for more info on this subject.) Among these EFA derivatives that some people may require from dietary sources are gamma-linolenic acid (GLA) and eicosapentaenoic acid (EPA).

3. Along with proteins, minerals, other lipids, and sugars, EFAs are building blocks of cell membranes and various internal cell structures.

4. EFAs are necessary for the metabolism and transportation of triglycerides and cholesterol.

5. EFAs are necessary for the development and the function of the human brain.

6. EFAs are necessary for proper function of the vision, nervous system, adrenal glands, and testes, playing a vital role in sperm formation and conception.

7. EFAs boost metabolism, metabolic rate, energy production, and oxygen uptake. Some researchers suggest EFAs are necessary in order for us to properly utilize sunlight.

8. EFAs, particularly Omega 3, have been shown to decrease growth of cancer cells, candida, and various anaerobic organisms destructive to the health of the human body.

9. In the November 1986 Journal of the National Cancer Institute, research indicated that Omega 3 and one of its derivatives as well as three of the derivatives of Omega 6 were seen to selectively destroy human cancer cells in tissue culture without damaging normal cells.

10. EFAs can be precursors to hormone like substances known as the prostaglandins. There are three main groups of these, which are known as **PG1s, PG2s, and PG3s**. Prostaglandins govern or influence many bodily processes including

platelet stickiness in the blood, arterial muscle tone, inflammatory response, sodium and fluid excretion through the kidneys, and immune function.

11. PG1s are derived from the Omega 6 family of fatty acids. Omega 6 (LA) can be changed into gamma-linolenic acid (GLA), which in turn can be changed into dihomo-gamma-linolenic acid (DGLA). PG1s are made from DGLA. PG1s prevent blood platelets from sticking together, assist in removing excess sodium as well as fluid, relax blood vessels, decrease inflammation, help insulin work more efficiently, benefit nerve function, regulate calcium metabolism, and improve immune function. People whose bodies do not efficiently make all of the above conversions may not manufacture sufficient PG1s from Omega 6 alone, but may require dietary sources of certain Omega 6 derivatives, most notably GLA.

12. PG2s are also derived from the Omega 6 family of fatty acids. As noted previously, LA can be converted into GLA, which can be converted into DGLA. DGLA in turn can be converted into arachidonic acid (AA). PG2s are derived from AA.

Different PG2s can either prevent or promote blood platelet aggregation. PG2s can promote water and sodium retention as well as inflammation. In general, PG2s oppose the PG1s, and are secreted in response to stress. Left unchecked, overproduction of PG2s can lead to all sorts of health problems associated with increased inflammation, decreased immune function, constricted blood vessels, increased sodium and fluid retention, and increased platelet stickiness. Some of the many health problems that may be associated with unchecked PG2 production in response to stress include cardiovascular disease, strokes, arthritis, high blood pressure, diabetes, and various immune disorders. One basic mechanism of keeping the PG2s in check is a PG1 known as **PGE1**, which slows the release of AA thus preventing its conversion into PG2s.

13. PG3s are made from the Omega 3 family of fatty acids. Certain fish oils are abundant sources of EPA. People whose bodies do not efficiently make all of the above conversions may require a dietary source of certain Omega 3 derivatives, most notably EPA. People whose ancestors consumed large amounts of EPA rich fish for

many generations often do not efficiently manufacture their own EPA and must rely upon a dietary source such as certain types of fish.

14. The ratio of Omega 6 to Omega 3 is also crucial, as excess Omega 6 as compared to Omega 3 promotes tumor formation. Research suggests that the ratio of Omega 6 to Omega 3 should be no greater than 5:1. Many experts suggest that the ideal ratio is as low as 2:1 or even 1:1 based on the ratio found in many healthy traditional diets. A typical ratio in most people's diets is in excess of 20:1. This is largely the result of increased consumption of various vegetable oils in the past century or so, most of which contain massive amounts of omega 6 and little or no omega 3.

15. Highly unsaturated fats are chemically unstable and thus highly prone to rancidity and other detrimental changes due to exposure to light, oxygen, or heat. This includes any rich source of EFAs and in fact any oil, whether from a plant or animal source. It is best to avoid any heated oils, or any oils that have had sufficient exposure to light, oxygen, or heat so as to damage them. For human consumption, oils need to be

processed and stored in a highly specific manner, and consumed fairly soon after pressing. Any deviation from these standards can pose some degree of health risk from their consumption. The modern diet contains a huge quantity of vegetable oils that have been exposed to light, oxygen, and heat. This poses a massive health risk to anyone consuming such a diet. No matter the quality of an oil in its ideal state, once exposed sufficiently to light, oxygen, or heat, it becomes detrimental to our health. For this reason, any cooking done with fats should be done with fats that are largely saturated such as coconut oil or ghee.

16. Both Omega 3 and 6 are extremely sensitive to deterioration in the presence of light, oxygen, and heat. Any or all of these will cause oil to go rancid very rapidly, thus making it of no benefit and, in fact, detrimental to the health of our bodies. For this reason it is imperative that oil be manufactured, processed, stored, and shipped in the utter absence of light, oxygen, and heat. There are seed oils available that meet these exacting standards. Certified organic seeds are processed, bottled and stored in the absence of light, oxygen, and heat. Any oils made from seeds or nuts

should be organic, as most pesticides are fat soluble and will therefore concentrate in the oil. Inert black plastic bottles are used which will not react with the oil. Any type of glass container, even dark brown glass, allows enough light in to cause rancidity. Indeed, of the three factors mentioned, light is by far the most detrimental, causing rancidity over 1000 times as rapidly as the next worse, which is oxygen. Inert gas is utilized during manufacture and bottling to insure the absence of oxygen. A special technology is utilized to maintain low temperatures (below 96 degrees F) during processing. Most so-called "cold-pressed" oils have reached temperatures of 160 degrees F or more as a result of friction during the extraction process. Once opened, a bottle should be kept refrigerated and used within two to four weeks ideally. Unopened bottles are best kept frozen. (Freezing may extend shelf-life of unopened bottles to six months or even longer, but we encourage you to treat this oil as the perishable item that it is for best results).

17. Fish oils are also highly vulnerable to detrimental transformation due to light, oxygen, and heat exposure during processing. Fish oils

from wild fish such as cod liver oil are the most abundant source of vitamin D by a wide margin. Yet there are legitimate concerns with the presence of various chemicals potentially found in fish oils. (Note: mercury is not fat soluble and hence not a specific concern with fish oil, yet there are numerous other contaminants which are legitimate concerns.) There are sources of cod liver oil from Iceland available which have been extensively tested and shown to have extremely low levels of these toxins as compared to other sources. Anyone consuming fish oils would be wise to investigate their own source for this reason and assure that it is the purest available.

4. Probiotics-

Probiotics assists digestion and assimilation of nutrients. Beta-Carotene is converted to Vitamin A in the intestine through the action of Lactobacillus for example. The lack of foul odour from stool and flatulence indicates a healthy balance of intestinal bacteria. When we begin to upgrade our nutritional program, or to cleanse and detox the body, it is advantageous to supplement higher levels of probiotics, followed by a maintenance level indefinitely. Reestablish intestinal flora with sufficient amounts of probiotics following the use of antibiotics which may kill both friendly and unfriendly bacteria. This also applies to natural antibiotics such as oregano and garlic. Drinking alcoholic beverages can also kill intestinal flora.

Twelve Points on Lactobacillus Acidophilus-

By John Ray ND

1. Lactobacillus bacteria are a group of aerobic, long, slender rods which produce large amounts of lactic acid in the fermentation of carbohydrates.

2. Daily dietary intake of Lactobacillus acidophilus helps maintain proper balance of healthy bacteria in the intestinal tract. (Some problems from a lack of "healthy" bacteria in the intestinal tract due to the proliferation of "unhealthy" bacteria are constipation, irritated colon and diarrhea. Acne, eczema and fever blisters may also be caused by "unhealthy" bacteria.

3. Lactobacillus acidophilus is essential to help synthesize and assimilate necessary vitamins in the intestinal tract.

4. Lactobacillus acidophilus has been found to help lower cholesterol levels in the blood stream.

5. Lactobacillus acidophilus has been known to help detoxify toxic and hazardous material found in the diet.

6. Lactobacillus acidophilus aids in producing enzymes which help the digestibility of food.

7. Lactobacillus acidophilus improves the digestibility of feed for animals and has been tested and used as a feed additive.

8. Lactobacillus acidophilus helps maintain the pH level of the intestine by producing lactic acid from carbohydrates thus preventing an increase of pH which could then allow the proliferation of sensitive microbes which could produce various toxic substances harmful to the health of the body.

9. Lactobacillus acidophilus helps to replace normal healthy bacteria in the gastrointestinal

tract after oral antibiotics have been administered. Oral antimicrobial drugs suppress the drug susceptible components of fecal flora (L. acidophilus) and thus allow, through increased pH, drug resistant strains to become predominant, resulting in loss of benefits derived from normal bacterial activity.

10. There is no known toxicity from ingesting too large a dose of Lactobacillus acidophilus.

11. Lactobacillus acidophilus in the intestinal tract are small in number compared to other organisms. It is, therefore, essential that the human body be assured a maintenance of the proper level of this particular culture by daily ingestion of Lactobacillus acidophilus.

12. Lactobacillus acidophilus is, therefore, justified as a supplemental dietary substance especially in these days when stress, uncertainty and unhealthy pollution of air, water and food predominate.

Aspartame/ Splenda: The poison to avoid

The chemical sucralose, marketed as "Splenda", has replaced aspartame as the #1 artificial sweetener in foods and beverages. Aspartame has been forced out by increasing public awareness that it is both a neurotoxin and an underlying cause of chronic illness worldwide.
"Splenda/sucralose is simply chlorinated sugar; a chlorocarbon. Common chlorocarbons include carbon tetrachloride, trichlorethelene and methylene chloride, all deadly. Chlorine is nature's Doberman attack dog, a highly excitable, ferocious atomic element employed as a biocide in bleach, disinfectants, insecticide, WWI poison gas and hydrochloric acid.
"Sucralose is a molecule of sugar chemically manipulated to surrender three hydroxyl groups (hydrogen + oxygen) and replace them with three chlorine atoms. Natural sugar is a hydrocarbon built around 12 carbon atoms. When turned into Splenda it becomes a chlorocarbon, in the family of Chlorodane, Lindane and DDT,

"It is logical to ask why table salt, which also contains chlorine, is safe while Splenda/sucralose is toxic? Because salt isn't a chlorocarbon. When molecular chemistry binds sodium to chlorine to make salt carbon isn't included. Sucralose and salt are as different as oil and water.
"Unlike sodium chloride, chlorocarbons are never nutritionally compatible with our metabolic processes and are wholly incompatible with normal human metabolic functioning. When chlorine is chemically reacted into carbon-structured organic compounds to make chlorocarbons, the carbon and chlorine atoms bind to each other by mutually sharing electrons in their outer shells. This arrangement adversely affects human metabolism because our mitochondrial and cellular enzyme systems are designed to completely utilize organic molecules containing carbon, hydrogen, oxygen, nitrogen, and other compatible nutritional elements.
"By this process chlorocarbons such as sucralose deliver chlorine directly into our cells through

normal metabolization. This makes them effective insecticides and preservatives. Preservatives must kill anything alive to prevent bacterial decomposition." Dr. Bowen believes ingested chlorocarbon damage continues with the formation of other toxins: "Any chlorocarbons not directly excreted from the body intact can cause immense damage to the processes of human metabolism and, eventually, our internal organs. The liver is a detoxification organ which deals with ingested poisons. Chlorocarbons damage the hepatocytes, the liver's metabolic cells, and destroy them. In test animals Splenda produced swollen livers, as do all chlorocarbon poisons, and also calcified the kidneys of test animals in toxicity studies. The brain and nervous system are highly subject to metabolic toxicities and solvency damages by these chemicals. Their high solvency attacks the human nervous system and many other body systems including genetics and the immune function. Thus, chlorocarbon poisoning can cause cancer, birth defects, and immune system destruction. These are well known effects of Dioxin and PCBs which are known deadly chlorocarbons. Just like aspartame, which was approval by the Food and Drug Administration when animal studies clearly demonstrated its toxicity- sucralose also failed in clinical trials with animals. Aspartame created brain tumors in rats. Sucralose has been found to shrink thymus glands (the biological seat of immunity) and produce liver inflammation in rats and mice. "We can expect to see a river of media hype expounding the virtues of Splenda/sucralose. We should not be fooled again into accepting the safety of a toxic chemical on the blessing of the FDA and saturation advertising. In terms of potential long-term human toxicity we should regard sucralose with its chemical cousin DDT, the insecticide now outlawed because of its horrendous long term toxicities at even minute trace levels in human, avian, and mammalian tissues. "Synthetic chemical sweeteners are generally unsafe for human consumption. This toxin was given the chemical name "sucralose" which is a play on the technical name of natural sugar, sucrose. One is not the other. One is food, the other is toxic; don't be deceived."

Dr. Bowen also calls attention to another seldom recognized and deadly permanent effect of these chemicals: "Aspartame, sold as NutraSweet, Equal and under other names, is a hypersensitization agent which causes Polychemical Sensitivity syndrome. Chlorocarbons strongly induce hypersensitivity diseases which are now becoming rampant."

James Bowen, M.D.

Food & Drink in the Modern World - Eating Clean

We have many considerations in this changing world in relation to food. Here are a few.

1. How the food is grown in relation to chemicals used. Non **GMO** that is not organic has high usage of toxic chemicals in production.

2. Has the food been grown with seed altered by genetic modifications? **GMO**

3. How is it processed and transported?

4. Where is it produced? Some countries have farming methods that are less than ethical, and have learned legal ways to export around the world. This is happening with many foods. Sometimes the label indicates where it was last packaged, not where it was produced.

5. Avoid fish high on the food chain such as tuna. Heavy metal accumulation is of great concern with our modern diet. Fish, especially tuna could have high mercury levels. Even fresh water fish

may have heavy metals contamination, and are to be avoided. Avoid all farmed fish.

6. Removing wheat, corn, rice and soy from the diet can significantly improve health by reducing inflammation. Replace with high quality whole food such as organic quinoa, hemp hearts, (refrigerate), and sprouted beans.

7. Remove canned food from diet. Buy food sold in glass containers, use glass (recycle) also for food storage. Plastic is to be avoided in all its forms. The petrochemical industry must be diminished and eventually given up for sustainable practices. Use a large mason jar for your water bottle. They are both durable and a healthier choice to plastic or metal.

Continuously upgrade and educate yourself on ever changing nutrition. Food that is prepared with unprocessed, whole and organic ingredients that have proven the test of time will help nourish and sustain vibrant health.

Eating Seasonally

Spring- Cleaning

Here in Canada rhubarb is a welcome spring food that wakes up the system into detox. Spring offers abundant nutrients the winter lacks. It is excellent for the body to go through the stages the seasons provide. Nettles, greens of all kinds, dandelion, asparagus etc. come into abundance in the spring. Growing herbs bring early welcome tastes that stimulate the palate, such as chives. As fruit and vegetables grow and ripen in your area, (as long as they are organic, and not grown by a road side) indulge heartily.

Summer- Light and Cool

Continue what is provided locally (farmers market), and keep heavy foods to a minimum. Foods that cool such as cucumbers and watermelon are excellent (organic of course). Tomatoes and basil pair beautifully, later in the season. Remain well hydrated especially in the warmer months.

Fall- Building Nutrients/Fat

Nuts and seeds: walnuts, pine nuts, cashew, pumpkin seed etc. provide nutrient dense and higher fat foods that are appropriate when preparing for winter. Warming foods such as yams and squash are easily digested. Curry meals with extra ghee is welcomed. Begin using fermented food such as sauerkraut from fall vegetables like cabbage. A little each day provides enzymes and probiotics as we eat more cooked food, especially in cold climates. I prepare a Chaga Chai tea that is excellent through fall and winter.

Winter- Sustaining

Root vegetables: beets, carrots, parsnips etc. and fruits that keep like apples sustain us though the darker and colder times when metabolism naturally slows. Fermented food and drinks each day through the winter month's keeps digestion on track. Soups and broth made with bones. Hearty stews. Quinoa, barley, dried beans and pulses are nourishing and warming. Spices such as; cayenne, cardamom, turmeric and ginger warm us in winter.

Celebrate with food and drink all year through.

Spilling the Beans

Genetically Engineered Foods May Cause Rising Food Allergies by James Bowen MD

seedsofdeception.com

Part 1: Genetically Engineered Soybeans

The huge jump in childhood food allergies in the US is in the news often, but most reports fail to consider a link to a recent radical change in America's diet. Beginning in 1996, bacteria, virus and other genes have been artificially inserted to the DNA of soy, corn, cottonseed and canola plants. These unlabeled genetically modified (GM) foods carry a risk of triggering life-threatening allergic reactions, and evidence collected over the past decade now suggests that they are contributing to higher allergy rates. Indeed, after the Canadian government announced in 2002 that they would "keep a careful eye on the health of Canadians" to see if GM foods had any adverse reactions, they abandoned their plans within a year, saying that such a study was too difficult. There is at least one protein in natural soybeans that has cross-reactivity with peanut allergies. That means that for some people who are allergic to peanuts, consuming soybeans may trigger a reaction. While it is certainly possible that the unpredicted side effects from genetic engineering soybeans might increase the incidence of this cross-reactivity, it is unlikely that any research has been conducted to investigate this. GM soy was introduced into the US food supply in late 1996. We are left only to wonder whether this had an influence on the doubling of US peanut allergies from 1997 to 2002. Eating GM foods is gambling with our health The introduction of genetically engineered foods into our diet was done quietly and without the mandatory labeling that is required in most other industrialized countries. Without knowing that GM foods might increase the risk of allergies, and without knowing which foods contain **GM** ingredients, the biotech industry is gambling with our health for their profit. This risk is not lost on everyone. In fact, millions of shoppers are now seeking foods that are free from any **GM** ingredients. Ohio-based allergy specialist John Boyles, MD, says, "I used to test for soy allergies all the time, but now that soy is genetically engineered, it is so dangerous that I tell people never to eat it—unless it says organic. Organic foods are not allowed to contain **GM** ingredients. Buying products that are certified organic or that say non-**GMO** are two ways to limit your family's risk from **GM** foods. A few food crops that have been genetically engineered: soy, corn, cottonseed, canola, Hawaiian papaya and some zucchini, bell peppers etc . This means avoiding soy lecithin in chocolate, corn syrup in candies, and cottonseed or canola oil in snack foods. Fortunately, the Campaign for Healthier Eating in America will soon make your shopping easier. This Consumer Non-**GMO** Education Campaign is orchestrating the clean out of **GM** ingredients from foods and the natural products industry. The campaign will circulate helpful non-**GMO** shopping guides to organic and natural food stores nationwide. The

Campaign will provide consumers with regular GM food safety updates that explain the latest discoveries about why, Healthy Eating Means No GMOs. - James Bowen MD

I lived in South West Ontario in a village on the same block as a mill where GMO corn and beans were processed. I lived there for 7 years. During this time my health declined and allergic reactions increased. The dust from the processing in the mill was everywhere even inside the house. When I moved and became more aware of gmo's and the chemicals used with this food production, I moved and adjusted my diet which changed my life. The unfortunate fact is that non gmo's are being produced in a non-organic way, and this required heavy chemical farming to produce. When shopping for non gmo's make sure it is organic as well.

Genetics and Nutrition

Our ancestor's give us a unique genetic make-up, that includes a historical predisposition in regards to nutrition. It is widely known that the First Nations- Native People of 'Turtle Island' (North

America) is under an epidemic of diabetes. The inability to process sugars, is an example of this. Alcohol, white flour, sugars, corn syrup/starch (in so many foods and drinks) etc. are destroying health for these people in early age. No one's heredity has prepared us for the overconsumption of sugars in today's modern diet. Yet, the First Nations are especially sensitive. I suspect from a traditional diet low in sugars and no alcohol. Consider our ancestors when choosing food and drink.

✧ Nourishing Traditions by Sally Fallon is an excellent resource.

Salt of The Earth

Good quality salt is vital to health.

'The body's interior ocean is salty, and without salt the myriad chemical reactions that support enzyme function, energy production, hormone production, protein transport and many other biochemical processes simply can't work. The chemical requirements of the human body demand that the salt concentration in the blood be kept constant. If the body does not get enough salt, a hormonal mechanism compensates by reducing the excretion of salt in the urine and sweat. But it cannot reduce this output to zero.

Western people today consume about half the amount of salt that they consumed traditionally. Before the days of refrigeration, most of our meat and fish was preserved by salting it. The Japanese, who have one of the highest salt intakes in the world, also have the highest life expectancy.

Salt provides two elements that are essential for life and for good health: sodium and chloride ions. They are both elements that the body cannot manufacture itself so it must be supplied by food.

A BRIEF HISTORY OF SALT

Demonization of a substance so vital to our health could only happen in a society ignorant of the history of salt. The use of salt by humans is intimately connected with our advance from a nomadic stone age life of hunting and gathering, to agriculture in which grain cereals became an important food. Salt is needed to make these foods taste good, and also to preserve meats and dairy foods for storage and transport. Increased use of salt led to increased production of glial cells in the brain, the cells that make us capable of creative thinking and long-term planning. Indeed, in ancient cultures, salt was considered the gift of the gods. Homer referred to salt as a "divine substance" and Plato described it as "especially dear to the gods." The Celtic word for salt meant "holy" or "sacred." The hunter gatherer obtains the salt he needs from the blood of animals (and sometimes the urine), which concentrate salt from the plants that they eat. Areas where there is very little sodium in the soil will support only small numbers of human beings.[7] The quest for salt led to the development of the major trade routes in the ancient world.'

> Weston Price Foundation-

Find an inland salt source that has a high mineral content, is environmentally clean, unbleached and without chemical processing. Nutritious salt is essential to health. Bolivian rose salt out of the

Andes Mountains is a high mineral, low sodium chloride uncontaminated example.

- Mineral Rich – High iron content gives Rose Salt its striking reddish hue; in addition to the iron compounds, Rose Salt also contains many other minerals that the human body needs including potassium, calcium and magnesium.

36% less sodium than regular table salt.

Nutritional Information for Bolivian Rose Salt:

Essential Minerals	Per 100 grams
Iron	3.3 mg
Potassium	432 mg
Calcium	477 mg
Magnesium	125 mg
Copper	.05 mg
Zinc	<.01 mg
Sodium	386 mg

Life Is Sweet~

- Keep it simple, keep it clean.
- Organic: maple syrup, raw unheated honey.

Avoid sugars derived from G.M.O. corn and beet, found in most prepared, packaged, restaurant/fast food, soft drinks, ice cream and candy. Keep a healthy limit on intake of foods high on the glycemic index such as potatoes (chips) corn (be aware of gluten free food being made from G.M.O. corn and rice), wheat, alcohol, many fruits and fruit juices, and their byproducts. This may sound simple but it isn't always easy. It took me over a year of vigilant effort to get through the initial cravings to unhealthy sugars. These sugars are food for the parasites, unhealthy bacteria, fungi and unfriendly yeast that proliferate in the gastrointestinal system. They cry out to be fed, (especially in the evening) creating an overwhelming urge to eat or drink something that turns to sugars. Probiotic intake is important here. This provides a flora for healthy bacterial balance. I take probiotics before bed, and mid-afternoon. This way they have less interference with digesting food.

Summation on Nutrition

- Research products, companies, farming methods, shipping methods and read labels. Words can be deceiving- like 'natural'.
- Hope Seeds is a great seed company in Eastern Canada. Here on Salt Spring Island, B.C. we have two companies devoted to seed saving, Eagleridge Seeds and Salt Spring Seeds.
- Grow a garden, even if it is a small container.
- High quality clean food sets the stage for celebration. This encourages slow savouring and development of the palate as well as aids optimal digestion. Food prepared with loving intent and shared with family and friends encourages an atmosphere of gratitude essential to good health.
- Whole food has not been heated, processed, changed in any way unless sprouted, soaked or fermented to enhance digestibility.
- Superfood has become a popularized word. It simply refers to nutrient dense food. Digestibility

and assimilation is worthy of consideration. Protein that is not digested efficiently causes stress on the entire body. Enzyme supplementation that is high in protease safeguards against undigested proteins. Some popular superfoods are Maca (Lepidium meyenii, known commonly as Peruvian Ginseng), Ashwaganda (*Withania somnifera* – Indian Ginsing), Goji berries, Pumpkin seeds, Chaga, Cacao…

- When choosing food and drink, consider 80+% to provide necessary nutrition. The rest may be considered treats.
- As Douglas Morrison writes in How We Heal, 'treat, don't cheat'. Attitude is important!
- Prepare at least 80% of your diet at home with ingredients you are aware of. Restaurant food kept to a minimum. A common sushi practice is adding white sugar while cooking the rice.
- Farmed salmon (what is served in most restaurants) as well as many wild species of fish may be contaminated with disease, heavy metals and radiation.

Green Drinks

Firstly, do not mix any fruit or fruit juices with protein or green drinks. This creates an acidic post digestion condition as the fruit digests faster turning to sugars. This may cause inflammation.

Dehydrated greens such as wheatgrass, barley greens etc. are completely acceptable if organic. Although fresh is preferable. A green drink may be sipped all day to provide balanced nutrition and energy. Chia, hemp hearts, flax and pumpkin seeds give texture and E.F.A.'s- ground fresh (ninja grinders work great).

Supplements

By providing daily the above regime of enzymes, minerals, probiotics, essential fatty acids and raw protein we are well on our way to a strong nutritional foundation. From here we add our supplements according. See your Naturopath, Nutritionist and/or wholistic practitioners for advice.

More physical considerations

- Maintain good posture.

- Stretch and strengthen with exercise you enjoy, preferably outdoors where air quality is high (trees). Breathe deeply and consciously.

- Keep bedroom free from electromagnetic pollution and radiation by keeping computers, phones and other devices far from the sleeping environment. Sleep and work as far away from wifi modems and smart meters as possible.

- Keep an open window while sleeping- air out the home regularly.

- Wholistic dentistry is an important consideration. Have mercury amalgam fillings removed safely. Hal Huggins devoted his life to this. His books are readily available.

- Save seeds- grow some of your own food.

In The Beginning

When upgrading your nutrition which includes reducing sugars from your diet you may experience cravings. The body seeks to come to a relative level of balance, yet that balance may be in the opposite direction to evolution. The healing crisis takes effort to get through. For example when someone quits smoking undesirable symptoms may be experienced that go away when you light up. With food the craving is the constant monkey on the back that we must be aware of, to continually make healthy choice. Cravings are caused by many factors. Here are a few.

-Trace mineral deficiency.

-Gastrointestinal parasites, bacteria, yeasts and fungi that feed on sugars.

-Bio-chemical addiction to certain food and drink.

-Poor digestion and assimilation of nutrients.

-Emotional trauma resulting in addiction.

In my experience both personally and professionally it is usually a combination of the above causes of craving or compulsive eating and drinking. In any case, to first apply physical principles corrects over time the physiology, and primes one for emotional work. Physical health lays the foundation to emotional, mental and spiritual health.

On Radiation

This is of great concern in this day and age. The sightless, odourless pollution we absorb though our skin, breathe, eat and drink is affecting our health detrimentally. Cell phones, cell towers, wifi etc. is silently affecting all life. The pollution from the Fukishima nuclear tragedy continues to pour into the Pacific Ocean, and into the air.

12 Points on RADIATION

Written and compiled by Dr John Whitman Ray N.D., M.D. (M.A.)

from "Patient's Guide to Body Electronics" by Dr. John Whitman Ray (1994)

1. The future is determined by our actions of the present and our consciousness which determines our choice of action. It has been established beyond reasonable doubt that there does exist a serious problem regarding the disposal of nuclear waste. It has been established by prominent scientists, beyond reasonable doubt, that the nuclear testing, nuclear accidents, nuclear generators, and nuclear waste have already contaminated the atmosphere, the water, the earth and all living things on our planet.

This contamination is protected by those in power to continue for many years. It is already known and acknowledged that the contamination which has already occurred may take 1000's of years to correct, as the problem currently exists. Just the recognition and consideration of the fact that there is no known method to correct the current amount of nuclear contamination in the world today justifies our taking immediate action to bring about an immediate and permanent cessation of the continued use of any form of atomic or nuclear energy.

2. It is understood that massive resistance shall arise from that segment of the elite who are motivated by economic profit and are dedicated to the perpetuation of the use of nuclear energy, even though the continuation of nuclear energy will gradually result in nuclear waste buildup. Long term problems are ignored in favor of short term profits at the expense of the safety of future generations. Yet, we the people have ascertained that greater importance is to be focused on the preservation of our genetic pool which preserves the perpetuation of both our plant and animal life and also shall ensure the perpetuation of the human species. The preservation of the genetic pool shall take precedence, without exception, over any motive which is concerned with financial profit and investment. The arms of all intelligent beings with long range vision, as compared to short range expediency for purpose of profit, are raised collectively in indignation against those

who continue the use of any form of nuclear power or energy. These same citizens collectively demand that governmental powers protest against those who perpetuate irresponsibly the continued use of nuclear energy, a sacrilege to those who value the sacredness of life. The people therefore shall speak out and demand appropriate governmental action from those who represent them.

3. It is understood that massive resistance shall arise from those who believe and promote nuclear energy as a preventive ingredient or deterrent for the prevention of war. It is therefore deemed necessary by the candid and comprehensive mind that we as a people must change our direction from planning for war and the prevention of war which in itself contributes to the cause of war, to thinking and planning for peace. History has taught us this lesson well. Have we forgotten so soon, that black mark against mankind which we choose not to remember, Hiroshima and Nagasaki, where on the 6th and 8th of August, 1945, 80,000 and 40,000 lives were instantly terminated, and 100,000's more died from radiation and sickness due to excessive radiation

exposure. Many more lived for a time to bear the scars and emotional illness which originated from that one moment of obliteration to oblivion.

4. If ever we were to arrive at a time when a nuclear war would take place, it is obvious that no one would win as the after effects shall be so devastating that it would take mankind 1000's of years to recover, if due to mutational factors, recovery would be possible at all. Much has been stated concerning the prospects of nuclear winter from which mankind would take 1000's of years to recover, if at all.

5. Let us assume that we do have a genuine concern for our future generations. If this is so, then we shall do everything in our power to prevent the continuing contamination of our genetic pool which is contributing to the increase in genetic mutations, no matter how subtle.

6. Greenpeace, an international association, staffed with a team of competent scientists, has recently conclusively indicated that scientific tests of water beyond the 12 mile limit at the Mururoa atoll in French Polynesia, is contaminated by nuclear material which is emanating radiation.

ANY EXISTING CONTAMINATION AND THE POSSIBILITY OF ADDING TO THE EXISTING CONTAMINATION BY ANY MEANS, AND ATTEMPTING TO COVER UP AND SUBVERT THIS INFORMATION BY FEEDING FALSE OR MISLEADING INFORMATION TO THE PEOPLE, IS IRRESPONSIBILITY IN THE EXTREME.

THE PEOPLE HAVE THE RIGHT TO BE MADE AWARE OF NUCLEAR CONTAMINATION THAT THEY MAY THEN HAVE THE RIGHT TO CHOOSE

Who knows the long term consequences of genetic mutation that will result from continued exposure to nuclear contamination in both plant and animal species? Every effort must be expended to protect that which we for so long have taken for granted.

7. It has been proven beyond reasonable doubt that health factors concerning both animal and vegetable life are directly related to the irreversible damaging effect of nuclear contamination. How much longer are we, as responsible leaders and contributors to the welfare of mankind, going to allow this insult to human, animal and vegetable life to continue?

8. For many years, psychologists have been aware of people who seem to have self-destructive tendencies. *We must address and transmute these patterns.*

9. All nuclear or atomic energy results in nuclear contamination.

THERE IS NO SAFE LEVEL OF NUCLEAR CONTAMINATION.

An established fact which leaves no doubt is that there is no safe level of nuclear contamination. Scientists, admittedly, acknowledge that there has not been devised a safe method of disposal for atomic or nuclear waste. Any disposal methods have only indicated problems that our future generations shall inherit for 1000's of years to come, with no solution offered.

10. This planet is our home. We cannot allow it to be contaminated and then move on to another home. Another home is not available. This home is our responsibility to care for and maintain. This is our inheritance and shall be the inheritance of our children and our children's children. Are we going to allow thoughtless men who have no

concern for the future to continue to irreversibly contaminate our home, or are we going to forcibly demand that this folly end immediately? What would we do if some stranger came into our home and took petrol or gasoline and poured it all over our belongings and then took a match and lit it?

Nuclear contamination is a ticking time bomb that is already slowly exploding. We have not yet seen the silent and deadly long term effects. We are now capable and determined to take appropriate and widespread action **NOW** and are determined to prevent the continuation of this intrusion into our lives and the lives of our future generations.

11. The time has come to take action from all fronts, including economic and political, to stop the continued use of any form of atomic or nuclear energy. The profit motive is no ldnger acceptable in any form to an enlightened citizenry. The ploy of peace preservation and the associated motives is unacceptable in any form to sensitive and intelligent souls. The private right of each country to nuclear testing has proven that:

None are exempt from the contamination of any type of testing or contamination from any type of use of nuclear materials.

12. Allowing misguided scientists and irresponsible unthinking leadership to continue in their activities without applying diligently due economic and political pressure is a distinct violation of the trust the people have placed in their political leadership. The power of political leadership always comes from the people who entrusted them to power, therefore the leader is always accountable to those who have entrusted him with this power, and have the responsibility of properly representing them and their rightful requests.

The only simple solution is to end immediately all use of nuclear energy and then to let things settle out or seek their own level of activity so that more attention can be placed on resolving differences between all types of life styles, religions, customs, temperaments, racial considerations, etc. within a structure protecting all people with their right to the exercise of conscience within a framework of "Unity in Diversity". Within this framework shall exist the protection of all mankind in the free expression of their individual rights as long as they do not interfere with the individual rights of others. The future will vindicate our determined actions of today.

DR. WALTER RUSSELL AND LAO RUSSELL FROM THE BOOK, ATOMIC SUICIDE:

'THE ISSUE CONCERNING THE USE OF ATOMIC OR NUCLEAR ENERGY CANNOT BE SEPARATED FROM THE ISSUE OF RESPECT FOR THE FREE WILL OR FREE AGENCY OF MAN. THE EARTH IS SMALL AND OUR INDIVIDUAL ACTIONS NOW AFFECT ALL 0N THE PLANET. WE ARE NO LONGER ALONE AND CANNOT CONSIDER OURSELVES ALONE, AS WHAT ONE PERSON DOES TODAY AFFECTS THE WHOLE OF SOCIETY. WE MUST NOW LEARN TO WORK IN CONCERT, ONE WITH ANOTHER. PRESSURE MUST BE APPROPRIATELY BROUGHT TO BEAR ON ALL THOSE WHOSE INDIVIDUAL ACTIONS AFFECT ADVERSELY THE WELFARE OF THE WHOLE.'

I now leave this issue in your hands, where does exist the power to act, as representatives of the people, for the ultimate interest of those future unborn whose ancestors have entrusted you with the opportunity to serve.

Respectively Submitted,

John Whitman Ray, N.D., M.D. (M.A.)

The Five Platonic Solids

The geometries nested here are known as the building blocks of creation. Vibrational frequency (energy), coming into physical form. We may observe this as the crystalline structure seen in water, salt, minerals, etc. Tourmaline for example, has a natural tetrahedral formation. This is considered connected with the element of fire. Fluorite has a natural octahedral formation and is linked to air. The cube as seen is pyrite is connected with the element of earth. Icosahedron is water's geometrical formation. Dodecahedron is related to the element of ether or spirit. I find this a fascinating study on the creation process, which helps us to understand our nature/consciousness. The Fibbanacci sequence is a mathematical formulation of how nature (energy) moves in the creation process. The nautilus shell is a good visual example of this, as are sunflowers. The mathematic sequence is 1+1=2, 2+1=3, 3+2=5, 5+3=8, 8+5=13, 13+8=21, 21+13=34, 34+21=55, 55+34=89, 89+55=144 ….into infinity.

The understandings of physics are naturally changing with continued conscious awakenings.

Emotion-Doorways to Change

The Art of Asking

Asking is paramount to change. Change of consciousness requires several aspects- it begins with formulating a question. Suppressed/resisted experience, and the denial we created those experiences can hinder humility. Humility begins with the realization of this. Then the asking/true seeking within begins. Consciousness changes as we apply the universal laws of Creation/Uncreation. "Ask and ye shall receive". When you ask- you are saying you are ready to receive. Be mindful of what, when, who and why- the motivations behind asking. It is a sacred act.

Suppression is held in the physical/emotional/mental/spiritual unconscious. As the suppression gradually releases to the emotional awareness we begin to feel what's there, and vent. Venting is a necessary part of the transmutation process.

Venting/allowing the expression of emotion is in no way projection upon anyone or anything. Following sufficient venting (intensified and held) we then move to control (contain) the emotion within. Holding the emotion intensely without emoting, then the feeling of the emotion will increase. If this occurs and we enthusiastically contain the emotion within, encompass in unconditional love, forgiveness and gratitude for the experience. We then experience a thorough transmutation and rapid upscale emotional movement. If there isn't an increase of intensity of the present emotion when we contain (control) then we go back to venting. When the three physical principles are applied, nutrition, stillness, breath, then the opening of the suppressed emotion begins. The emotional and physical bodies are directly connected. They affect each other continuously. The energy of the emotional body usually moves and changes from the bottom up. The root center resonates with unconsciousness. Unconsciousness is all things we are unaware of. This includes suppressed emotion, memory with associated words we were unable to experience in the moment that it occurred. This is a natural defense mechanism, when something experienced is resisted. When we make the choice to change, suppressed emotion will surface to be released. There are three main aspects to discover.

- Word pattern
- Emotion
- Memory

When all three are present, they may be released by applying one or more of 'the three powers'.

- Forgiveness
- Love
- Gratitude

This process requires commitment and an increasing willingness to face one's own emotional wounds and traumas. Self-compassion and support are extremely important here.

- Willingness to change, willingness to feel, and a willingness to let go.
- Own and maintain emotional responsibility. Non projection.
- Feel what we feel WITH love, gratitude and or forgiveness. *The Three Powers.

These points are key components to emotional transmutation. Welcome the emotion like an old friend. This energy is present and creating our experience in an unconscious way. By making it conscious, we are then in a position to release the stagnant energies. Changing emotional consciousness requires ever increasing self-responsibility, avoiding blame or justifications. When an outer circumstance triggers a reactive emotional response, be aware of the presence of the three powers. Recognize the trigger as our opportunity to see/feel a pattern of emotion present within, shown for our perusal and edification. Practice gratitude for the triggers. Keep the emotion close without projection on anything or anyone external. Observe the internal process. Observe the words that accompany the emotion. When we are aware of what is there, from here it may be changed. Transmuted emotional energy provides the whole system with the opportunity for renewed capacity.

When we find ourselves in emotional reactivity in daily life, have compassion for self, forgiveness for self, love for self, then extend that to all.

Addiction-Habits-Self Medication

The unconscious program to suppress stress and emotion can stimulate the compulsion to self-medicate. Food, caffeine, sugar, tobacco, alcohol, recreational drugs, exercise, internet, sex… the list goes on. Discontinuing unhealthy habits and addiction may require professional assistance.

"Self-medication involves the suppression of discomfort by moving ourselves down to a lower level of balance and comfort. In regards to both sugar and alcohol, two of the most common forms of self-medication, is highly influenced by the individual's nutritional status." How We Heal pg. 414

As we improve our nutrition we experience less and less desire to self-medicate. This takes continuous efforts and perseverance.

Emotional Body Construct

Seven energy centers within the human body correspond to physical organs. These centers are where the emotional body concentrates its energy. Each emotional center contains all seven levels of emotion, nested in spheres equaling 49. The awareness of emotional levels increases exponentially with upscale movement from level 7 (unconsciousness) to level 1 (enthusiasm/love). At the top of each level is the access point to that level of love, which is accessible to transmute all beneath it.

Qualities of the Emotional Centers

- Level 1~ Love- Enthusiasm & Creativity
  -feeling love~ accessible at all 7 levels, with the power to transmute all levels of emotionality beneath it.
  Corresponds with the pineal gland

- Level 2~ Emotional Pain~ Unity
  -see/feel multidimensional viewpoints.
  Corresponds with the pituitary gland

- Level 3~ Anger~ Truth
  - power and control- (mastery of)
    Corresponding with the thyroid/parathyroid glands

- Level 4~ Fear~ Freedom
  - becoming aware of choice.
    Corresponds with the heart/thymus

- Level 5~ Grief~ Joy
  - the feeling of loss/victimization- 'why me'.
    Corresponds with the pancreas/adrenals

- Level 6~ Apathy~ Compassion
  - the feeling of 'who cares'.
    Corresponding with the spleen

- Level 7~ Unconsciousness~ Self Awareness
  - black/white, right/wrong, all or nothing.
    Corresponding with the gonads,(testes in male, ovaries in female)

Recognize patterns of behavior as related to the emotional qualities. All levels are interconnected, making a flow of upward energy within the body.

Summation on Emotional Transmutation

- Choose a private environment.
- Sit or lay with the spine straight.
- Breathe deeply and evenly without pause.
- Remain perfectly still.
- Welcome the emotional energy.
- Take whatever you find and work with that.
- Do not involve others, blame or project upon anyone or anything- overtly or covertly (silently).
- Be willing to intensify the feeling and allow it to last as long as it needs to be felt.
- Now feel the emotion with Love. If you cannot access Love, feel with forgiveness for self and/or others. If you cannot access Forgiveness, feel with Gratitude. If you cannot access any of the three powers, feel how you feel about the emotion. For example, you may feel ashamed of the anger, afraid of the pain, so feel that, see if you can love that, forgive that, be grateful for that. It will unravel in this way back to the core emotion, where you will again have the opportunity to feel with Love, Forgiveness and Gratitude.

- Attachment to outcome such as how, when, what; may distract the process. Be alert to expectations, doubt, disappointment, etc., transmuting as they arise. When emotional pain is accessed and transmuted with some degree of enthusiasm/love, we access the mental body at that level of progression. At this specific level we begin to see 'both' sides of a resisted duality. This is considered entering the mental body. The word pattern and memory are present here.
- Bring the three creative energies together simultaneously, release with forgiveness, love and gratitude. This is full transmutation. This takes perseverance. The further up we go on the emotional scale, the more expanded the awareness of the mental body. Here is where meditation and exercise in focused concentration becomes increasingly important. As we move emotionally upscale, we become increasingly sensitive, and aware.
- Enjoy that.

Higher and Lower Law

Simplistically speaking emotional law is higher than physical law, mental higher than physical and emotional, and spiritual law higher than them all. The paradox is physical law must be observed and maintained to be aware of the higher laws of emotion. Emotional law must be maintained to observe the mental law, etc. Within emotion, there are higher and lower law, and this becomes more and more complex before coming into simplicity. This may be observed as a sine wave. From unconsciousness to fear, we move from simplicity to complexity. From fear to enthusiasm we move from complexity into higher levels of simplicity. Now apply this within each level, 7X7.

When emotion is transmuted it has the capacity to transmute emotions beneath (see scale of emotion). Enthusiasm (love) is at the top of each emotional level x 7. When accessed and applied to transmutation this effects all emotion under that particular level. Coldness sometimes occurs in and around the body. This can be explained in terms of atomic endothermic reaction. (see How We Heal, 363-64) Simplistically, the body is using

energy (drawing it in) to change it into something else. (biological transmutation). The atomic exothermic reaction is experienced as heat in and around the body. The body is releasing energy. More on this provided in depth, with the writings in the Logic in Sequence series by John Whitman Ray, founder of Body Electronics.
These three books are out of print yet may be found on my site free of charge.

The Mental Body - Transmutation & Visualization

As the emotional body (specifically pain at level 6 within all 7 levels of emotion) opens and clears with transmutation, we become aware of an increased ability to see from the mental body. Inner visualization becomes clear, in colour, motion picture, auditory, a full inner sensory experience. This is natural as pain is released, and the pineal functions more fully. Moving to transmute the mental body prior to emotional transmutation is futile. From the mental body we begin to see how we created our individual life experience. Patterns of thought (that became experience) become clear. From here mental transmutation is possible. We gain access to the mental body incrementally, with upscale transmutation of emotion. This is a universal 'fail safe'. With this awareness, focus to the encompassment of a specific dualistic pattern, using inner sight, accessing and directing the violet light brings the patterns of the mental body into harmony.

Encompassment of Duality is applied (holding both sides with focused concentration), while accessing and directing the Violet Flame, until the duality experienced with equanimity on both sides. This allows the reconnection of the duality in perfect harmony.

The duality being observed and transmuted will gradually become a harmonious interplay.

Summation on Mental Transmutation-

- Inner sight- awareness of the duality (both sides of a pattern).
- Encompassment of the specific pattern holding both sides.
- Awareness of the violet light/fire.
- Bring both sides together while allowing.
- Make it happen/let it happen simultaneously.
- Stay with it to completion/harmonization.
- This practice requires focused concentration.
- At this point we are practicing physical, emotional and mental principles simultaneously.

- Increased self-responsibility is natural as we become increasingly aware of our capacity to create and un-create.
- Intuition gradually returns to awareness.
- Transmutation changes consciousness in an evolutionary way.
- Regeneration/healing is a pleasant side effect of consciousness change.

Higher and lower law becomes increasingly apparent as we move upscale and have greater and greater access to the mental body, from where thought/inner vision views our creative experience. The bottom up approach as outlined here begins with applying physical application, that naturally supports emotional opening- emotional transmutation clears the way for mental awareness. The practice of mental principles brings one to spiritual awareness from where spiritual harmony exists always.

Every effort we make in the evolutionary path is not lost.

Spirit~

Spirit contains pure creative potential.
As human beings we are interfacing within the wholistic construct of nature that came into molecular structure via spirit/energy. The physical experience is fully equipped with the spiritual capacity for conscious evolution. It is how we choose to live that determines the speed and depth of the evolutionary process. As we consistently practice the release of anything less than love we realize the immense spiritual support. I have found inner asking for guidance and understanding of great blessing. Some call this prayer.

Listening- practicing awareness of the internal and external environment- paying attention with the constant willingness to apply the 'laws' of love, light and perfection.

The Three Powers

Creating a sacred space where you may privately practice transmutation and meditation is important to build the habit and energy.

- Meditate in the energy of unconditional love.
- Meditate in the energy of gratitude.
- Meditate in the energy of unconditional forgiveness.

Allow these energies to move through your body- they will radiate naturally in the auric field when integrated physically. Daily practice of this assists to maintain alignment in the emotional body as well as strengthens the ability to respond appropriately. Response ability.

Independent practice of evolutionary principles, deepen our inner journey. Gradually and sometimes suddenly, remembering our connection with all that is.

Kriya Yoga

"The word yoga itself means union of the individual consciousness with the Universal Consciousness or Spirit. Yoga is a profound science of unfolding the infinite potentials of the human mind and soul."

~Paramahansa Yogananda
Author of Autobiography of a Yogi

Illia Heart~

In her early years Illia was influenced greatly by her maternal Grandmother, her name was Velma. As a young woman she owned and operated a health food store, a metaphysical book shop and later a wholistic health centre.

Illia raised four children who are all of good heart.

She spent nine years in concentrated study and practice of Kriya Yoga, from 1988- 1997. At this time she earned a degree in Ayurveda. She taught numerous workshops on Yogic Tradition and health in Toronto, Canada during this time. She continues in this Yogic lineage.

In 1999 she began many years of study in the field of Body Electronics. Douglas Morrison certified Illia as a Body Electronics Instructor in 2003. She has taught yearly B.E. Intensives since this time.

Drunvalo Melchizedek certified Illia as a teacher of Awakening The Illuminated Heart in 2011 after 10 years of study and practice of his work. Earth/Sky, Flower Of Life, Living In The Heart as well as participating in Ceremony in Peru with Drunvalo were influential in Illia's evolution.

Ceremony and Oral Tradition as shared by Elders of Turtle Island contributes greatly to her awareness and understandings of life.

Presently Illia resides on Salt Spring Island, B.C., Canada where she operates Illia's- Body Mind Spirit. Her love of Stones has increased the business to provide quality Stones and Crystals.

She teaches workshops on wholistic practice and holds Body Electronic Intensives.

"Self-Realization is an inner process of continuous discovery and conscious change."

Illia

Great Spirit-

Bless us as we celebrate life on this great planet, may we do so in grace. May we be good brothers and sisters, assisting each other to live happy healthy lives. May we see the integral part we play, on earth and in the heavens-

giving and receiving joyfully.

From our heart we give thanks.

We are all related.

Printed in Great Britain
by Amazon